MEMPHIS GRIZZLIES
ALL-TIME GREATS

BY DAVID J. CLARKE

Copyright © 2024 by Press Room Editions. All rights reserved. No part of this book may be used or reproduced in any manner whatsoever, including internet usage, without written permission from the copyright owner, except in the case of brief quotations embodied in critical articles and reviews.

Book design by Jake Slavik
Cover design by Jake Slavik

Photographs ©: Jeff Chiu/AP Images, cover (top), 1 (top); Jim Mone/AP Images, cover (bottom), 1 (bottom); Matt A. Brown/Icon Sportswire/AP Images, 4; Jill Connelly/AP Images, 6; Alan Spearman/AP Images, 8; Tyler Kaufman/AP Images, 10; Brandon Dill/AP Images, 12, 21; Alex Goodlett/AP Images, 15; Brian Rothmuller/Icon Sportswire/AP Images, 16; Charles Krupa/AP Images, 18

Press Box Books, an imprint of Press Room Editions.

ISBN
978-1-63494-663-6 (library bound)
978-1-63494-687-2 (paperback)
978-1-63494-734-3 (epub)
978-1-63494-711-4 (hosted ebook)

Library of Congress Control Number: 2022919278

Distributed by North Star Editions, Inc.
2297 Waters Drive
Mendota Heights, MN 55120
www.northstareditions.com

Printed in the United States of America
Mankato, MN
082023

ABOUT THE AUTHOR

David J. Clarke is a freelance sportswriter. Originally from Helena, Montana, he now lives in Savannah, Georgia, with his golden retriever, Gus.

TABLE OF CONTENTS

CHAPTER 1
GRIZZLY BEGINNINGS 4

CHAPTER 2
GRIT 'N' GRIND 10

CHAPTER 3
NEW HEIGHTS 16

TIMELINE 22
TEAM FACTS 23
MORE INFORMATION 23
GLOSSARY 24
INDEX 24

CHAPTER 1
GRIZZLY BEGINNINGS

The NBA brought in two new teams in 1995. Both were in Canada. The Toronto Raptors played in the East. The Vancouver Grizzlies represented the West.

Vancouver struggled for several years. The team had few star players. Its first draft pick in 1995 was 7'2" **Bryant Reeves**. The 275-pound center was known as "Big Country." The nickname was in part due to his size. But it was also because he grew up in a tiny town in Oklahoma. Reeves averaged 12.5 points per

game over six seasons. However, back injuries ended his career.

A year after taking Reeves, Vancouver selected **Shareef Abdur-Rahim** in the draft. The forward was the opposite of Reeves. Abdur-Rahim was a slender, quick scorer. He led the team in points in each of his five seasons with Vancouver.

The Grizzlies never made the playoffs in any of their six years in Vancouver. In 2001, the team moved to Memphis. The Grizzlies' first star in Memphis was flashy point guard **Jason Williams**. He entertained fans with no-look and behind-the-back passes.

STAT SPOTLIGHT

POINTS IN A SEASON
GRIZZLIES TEAM RECORD

Shareef Abdur-Rahim: 1,829 (1997-98)

ICED OUT

The Grizzlies had the second pick in the 1999 draft. They used it on Steve Francis, a point guard from the University of Maryland. However, Francis had already told the team he would not move to Vancouver. The Grizzlies were forced to trade Francis to the Houston Rockets.

Center **Pau Gasol** caught many of those passes. Gasol came to the team in a 2001 trade for Abdur-Rahim. The big man from Spain was a good scorer and rebounder. Gasol scored with ease in the paint. He made more than half of the shots he took while he played for Memphis. The big man was also a skilled passer. Williams and Gasol led Memphis to the playoffs for the first time in 2003–04. But the Grizzlies lost their opening series without winning a game.

CHAPTER 2
GRIT 'N' GRIND

The Grizzlies eventually traded Pau Gasol to the Los Angeles Lakers in 2008. One of the players who came back in the deal was his younger brother.

Marc Gasol helped bring in the "Grit 'n' Grind" era of Grizzlies basketball. The team played a physical style and wore opponents down. Gasol was a strong defender. He was

> **STAT SPOTLIGHT**
>
> **CAREER REBOUNDS**
> GRIZZLIES TEAM RECORD
> Marc Gasol: 5,942

named the NBA Defensive Player of the Year in 2012-13. His tough play is also how he got the nickname "Wendigo." That is a mythical monster known for eating people whole.

Gasol shared the post with a bruising forward. **Zach Randolph** stood 6'9" and weighed 250 pounds. "Z-Bo" was tough to stop near the basket. He used his big frame to average a double-double over the course of eight seasons with the Grizzlies. The forward made two All-Star teams with Memphis. Randolph was also a beloved member of the community. He often helped struggling families. Randolph's No. 50 was retired by the team in 2021. That made him the first Grizzlies player to have his number retired.

COACH HOLLINS

The coach of the Grit 'n' Grind Grizzlies was Lionel Hollins. The former NBA guard started as an assistant with the team in Vancouver in 1995-96. Hollins became the head coach in 2009. His final season coaching Memphis was 2012-13. He led the Grizzlies to 56 wins that year.

In the backcourt Memphis was led by another rugged player. Point guard **Mike Conley** rarely missed a game. Even a broken facial bone didn't keep him out long. That injury forced Conley to miss three games. He spent 12 seasons in Memphis. He helped the Grizzlies make the playoffs in seven of those seasons. Conley's 788 games played are the most in team history.

Tony Allen was the team's other key guard. Allen didn't score much. But he was one of the toughest defenders in the league. Great NBA scorers like Kobe Bryant and Kevin Durant called Allen the hardest defender they ever had to play against.

JACKSON JR.
13

CHAPTER 3
NEW HEIGHTS

The Grit 'n' Grind Grizzlies were gone by 2020. But a new set of young players was taking over in Memphis. A few bad seasons had given the Grizzlies some high draft picks.

Center **Jaren Jackson Jr.** was the fourth pick in the 2018 draft. "Triple-J" could score, but he was an even better defender. Jackson led the NBA in blocked shots in 2021–22.

STAT SPOTLIGHT

BLOCKS IN A SEASON
GRIZZLIES TEAM RECORD
Jaren Jackson Jr.: 177 (2021–22)

The Grizzlies took guard **Ja Morant** with the second pick in the 2019 draft. The 6'3", 175-pound floor leader was the NBA Rookie of the Year in 2019–20. The last Grizzly to win that award had been Pau Gasol in 2001–02. Morant quickly proved to be one of the most exciting players in the league. He drove to the basket at will. And those drives usually ended with a highlight dunk or layup. Morant scored 27.4 points per game in 2021–22.

LATE BLOOMER

Ja Morant was only 5'9" when he started high school in Sumter, South Carolina. He couldn't even dunk until his senior year. And few colleges wanted him. Morant ended up playing at little-known Murray State University in Kentucky. In his sophomore season, Morant averaged 24.5 points per game along with 10.0 assists and 5.7 rebounds.

Morant and Jackson led the Grizzlies to a 56–26 record that season. But other players helped, too. Swingman **Dillon Brooks** was a clutch scorer. He also annoyed opponents with physical defense.

Desmond Bane came to the Grizzlies in a trade during the 2020 draft. The shooting guard started 17 games as a rookie. But in 2021–22, he started all 76 games he played. He also doubled his scoring to 18.2 points per game. Bane set a new team record with 228 three-pointers made during the season. He then broke the team's playoff record by hitting 43 in the postseason.

Memphis lost in the second round of the 2022 playoffs. But Morant and the rest of the team looked set to compete for championships very soon.

TIMELINE

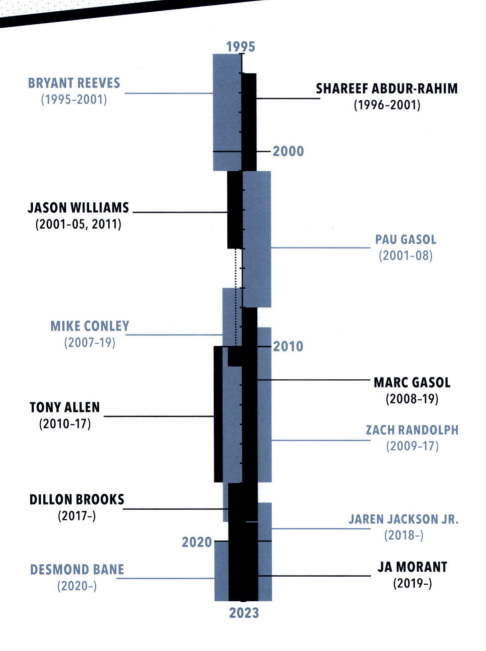

TEAM FACTS

MEMPHIS GRIZZLIES

Formerly: Vancouver Grizzlies (1995–2001)

First season: 1995-96

NBA championships: 0*

Key coaches:

   Lionel Hollins (1999-2000, 2004-05, 2008-09 to 2015-16)

      214-201, 18-17 playoffs

   Taylor Jenkins (2019-)

      128-99, 7-10 playoffs

MORE INFORMATION

To learn more about the Memphis Grizzlies, go to pressboxbooks.com/AllAccess.

These links are routinely monitored and updated to provide the most current information available.

*Through 2021–22 season

GLOSSARY

assists
Passes that lead directly to a teammate scoring a basket.

clutch
Successful late in games or in pressure-filled situations.

double-double
When a player reaches 10 or more of two different statistics in one game.

draft
An event that allows teams to choose new players coming into the league.

grit
Strength while facing adversity.

post
The area close to the basket where taller players usually set up.

rookie
A first-year player.

slender
Gracefully thin.

swingman
A player who can play both guard and forward.

INDEX

Abdur-Rahim, Shareef, 7, 9
Allen, Tony, 14

Bane, Desmond, 20
Brooks, Dillon, 20
Bryant, Kobe, 14

Conley, Mike, 14

Durant, Kevin, 14

Francis, Steve, 9

Gasol, Marc, 11–13
Gasol, Pau, 9, 11, 19

Hollins, Lionel, 13

Jackson, Jaren, Jr., 17, 20

Morant, Ja, 19–20

Randolph, Zach, 13
Reeves, Bryant, 5, 7

Williams, Jason, 7, 9